Mountain Mother Poems

poems by

Alice Teeter

Finishing Line Press
Georgetown, Kentucky

Mountain Mother Poems

Copyright © 2017 by **Alice Teeter**
ISBN 978-1-63534-151-5 First Edition
All rights reserved under International and Pan-American Copyright Conventions.
No part of this book may be reproduced in any manner whatsoever without written permission from the publisher, except in the case of brief quotations embodied in critical articles and reviews.

ACKNOWLEDGMENTS

Per Contra published: "The bucket," "Paths worn smooth," "Your mother's porch," "Your mother's view," "Fish," "Piano music," "Fake flowers I," "Rock face," "Light everywhere evenly at once," "Night," "Panes," "Stones"
The Southern Poetry Anthology, Volume V: Georgia, Texas Review Press also published "Stones."

Publisher: Leah Maines

Editor: Christen Kincaid

Cover Art: Traditional Chinese painting, Shao-Chun Wang © 123RF.com

Author Photo: Cinemadona Studios LLC

Cover Design: Elizabeth Maines McCleavy

Printed in the USA on acid-free paper.
Order online: www.finishinglinepress.com
    also available on amazon.com

Author inquiries and mail orders:
Finishing Line Press
P. O. Box 1626
Georgetown, Kentucky 40324
U. S. A.

Table of Contents

The bucket 1

Paths worn smooth 2

Lines and squares of light 3

Plenty 4

Darker than dark 5

Light streaming in the windows 6

The bouquet 7

Your mother's porch 10

Your mother's view 11

Fish 12

Empty 13

Notes 14

Fishing in early morning 15

Falling 16

Piano music 17

Fake flowers I 18

Two rivers 19

Rock face 20

Light everywhere evenly at once 21

Night 22

Panes 23

Stones 24

for Ann Doak Teeter and Minerva McGill Doak

The bucket

Your mother lives above you on the mountain,
around the hillside, many switchbacks away.
You haven't seen her for years although your
children used to visit when they were little.
Your youngest girl, the theoretical mathematician,
is the one who figured out the angles and the lengths
and what exactly it would take for your mother
to be able to drop a bucket down the slope
and knock it against your front door.
It was all right when she was there to read
the notes and do your mother's bidding,
but once the kids departed, you were left alone
with the thump, thump, thump on your door
once or twice a day—always something—
A pinch of salt, the newspaper.

Paths worn smooth

You walk this trail every day: it's the track
you used to go to visit your mother.
You've paced it so long that parts are slick,
smooth—down in the valley easy to use.
You've marched it in your sleep.

But most of it is treacherous,
full of drop-offs, boggy places
where you pick up huge clumps
of stones and mud on your shoes
that slow you to a standstill.

There's a weeping willow that whips you
when the wind is blowing hard
and that rock that juts out,
which you never see
and always hits you on the head.

You have other friends who live here
on this mountain. You'd like to find
a better road to visit them.
You tried different tracks before.
It's hard to see the traces of those paths.

You see a blackberry bush before you
and remember this is where a new trail started.
Through sweet berries and their thorns
you start uphill, push through the greenery,
spider webs and brambles, to find another way.

Lines and squares of light

You're thinking about going to see your mother.
The last time you saw her was right after
she'd added that wraparound porch to her house
up there high above you on this mountainside.

She wanted the garden hose attached to the tap,
twelve feet away through a small opening
the builders left for access—your job to hook it up.

You inserted the hose into your belt loop,
squeezed through the portal and crawled,
sawdust in lines matching gaps in the boards above,

the spigot glinted in the shadows. As you attached the hose,
you realized you'd always liked things easy,
your mother never seemed to mind things hard.

And then, as you turned back toward the opening, you wondered
how you had gotten through that small square of light
and how in the world you were going to get out.

Plenty

Sometimes when your mother wakes,
she cannot tell if it's dawn or dusk.
She has that many windows
and her house is that round.

Darker than dark

You pull in your driveway and look
at the black square of your house.

Above you on the mountain
your mother has all her lights on.

Light streaming in the windows

In your mother's house now sunlight streams in every window.
Her whole place is alight from porch to study to music room.
This house where you live, the one she grew up in,
it's still full of shadows from the overhanging trees
surrounding your little place on the mountainside.

You add illumination as best you can, but the oak trees
have their uses besides shade so you don't want to cut them
and you don't have the strength to move the mountains
that surround your house on all sides. You content yourself
with shades and shadows, track lighting in the living room.

At night in winter, the starlight shines in the windows
and sometimes you can see the Milky Way wheeling
through the heavens, but only if you hike to the overlook
on the dark side of the mountain and wait.
You're sure your mother can see it from her back yard.

In certain seasons the full moon rises between two hills
straight ahead. You track it until it moves behind you
out of sight behind this looming mountain you live on.
Most days you are too busy to notice the moon or the stars.
You leave for work early and come home late, head down.

Sometimes you walk in your house and you wonder
if this is how your mother felt living here. Did she
walk in the door and sink down into the shadows
onto the sofa? You know she did. You saw her sit
and read for hours under that lamp in the corner.

You have piles you move from one place to another.
Papers you've touched many times and never filed.
Today you want to go walking, but you've hurt your back.
All you can do is sit or lie down in the clutter and dream
that tomorrow you'll be out again moving in the sunlight.

The Bouquet

Up the mountain from you, your mother grows beautiful flowers
around her house. You've not seen your mother's garden in years,
but your daughter would tell you about it when
she came back from visiting. Your daughter who always
wondered what made you angry, the one who's doing something
with fractals, loved math from when she was young, the one who
figured out all the angles and what exactly it would take
for your mother to be able to drop a bucket down
from her balcony to knock against your front door.

One day you hear the crack of the bucket on your door.
You open expecting a request for salt or some magazine.
What you see right at eye level
is the most beautiful bouquet
you have ever seen in your whole life.
You close the door.

All day you do your chores, go out the back way to the car,
drive to town, eat supper, go to bed.

Early the next day you open the door and stare briefly.
Throughout the day you imagine the bucket of flowers
hanging there filling the whole doorway or
a small can with a few withered stalks drying in the wind.
Once in awhile you check your imagination with a glance.
That night you have crackers and milk.

The third day you open the door and leave it open.
The bucket hangs there, a morning breeze
blows the fragrance through the house.
In the afternoon you stick your finger in to check
the water level. You notice tiny white buttons
hidden in the dark green foliage deep inside the bunch.

Next dawn you open the door wide just as the sun
comes peeking up over the ridge, light
streams through the flowers dazzling your eyes.
You bring the bucket in and place it
on the dining room table, a dishtowel underneath
to protect the wood. The door and the table and the flowers
make a line into the kitchen where you work.

For three days the flowers sit on your table.
You work around them, eat at one end.
You notice the petals are beginning to drop.
The water smells green and murky.
You compost the flowers, pour the water
on your garden, wash the bucket, the dishtowel,
put them in the drainer to dry.

Your daughter phones that she is coming
for the weekend. You decide to bake snowflakes —
the family recipe passed down—
unsweetened chocolate melted first,
vanilla, sugar, eggs, a little salt, flour,
baking powder, some oil.
A bit of powdered sugar set aside.

You roll the dough into balls,
bits of darkness stick to your hands.
You notice how much your palms
look like your mother's used to, when.
Powdered sugar coats your fingertips.
Warm chocolate replaces the lingering smell of flowers.

Next morning you take a tea towel,
wrap up six snowflakes, place them
in the bottom of the bucket,
tuck in a paperback you've finished,
hang the bucket on the line
outside your front door,
pull once on the rope.

High above you hear a faint bell.
Later you hear one clunk —
the bucket hitting the eave as it rises.

Your mother's porch

Your mother's porch wraps around the house
on three sides; the veranda hangs over
the mountainside way up there,
high above your little house below.

When the fog rolls in,
it's like frosted glass
enclosing her porch;
water drips from the arms
of chairs, circles down the legs
and across the floor.

When she sings on those days,
there is no echo.
Her voice barely carries
beyond the wall of fog;
instead it drops down the slope
running in rivulets
between stones and
rhododendron roots
to pool at your front door.

Your mother's view

Your mother's view is wide—
a sweeping vista of the valley
with the lake down below,

she can see clouds rolling
across the face of the mountains
across the way, the hawks
ride the air currents—
distant specks.

You have the same view
only smaller, lower,
partially obscured by hillocks,
tall oak trees, with acorns
that drop onto your roof
with a bang.

Fish

In the bucket are fish
your mother caught in the pond
by her house above you on this mountain.

She must have been up early
to have caught so many.
You hear the silvery fish thrash
the water as the bucket descends
before you see what she has
lowered down to you with a note
taped to the side of the plastic pail
"clean all, send half back."

You had plans this morning.
You were going to weed the flowers
that grow alongside the front walk.

You lift the bucket off its hook.
Your mother high above you
feels the weight release.

Empty

Today your mother has lowered the bucket empty
it dangles at eye level, sways in the breeze
that is blowing around the mountainside you live on.

Every so often the beige pail jumps
as your mother tests the weight
to see if it's ready.

You have no idea what she wants.
You look around your kitchen —
scarcity stares back at you.

You pick up the paperback
you're halfway through
toss it in the bucket and tug.

Notes

Your mother stands on her porch
to sing. She tosses notes
down the mountainside.

They fall from her aerie
high above your little house
as she sends her voice out
across the valley.

They bounce back from the slope
across the way and create an echo,
a flurry of white cascades.

You stand in your tiny front yard
among the flowers in your garden;
the deluge washes your face.
This is the water you long for.

Fishing in early morning

Your mother fishes in her pond
in the early morning
when the owls have gone to bed.

She chases the eagles off
with shouts—flaps her apron,
stamps her feet,
until they spread their wings
and glide away.

If you were there,
she would have you do it.

Falling

Your mother knows secret places
on this mountain—spaces
you've never seen.
She told you about them—spots
she explored alone as a child.

The cave deep and low where
she slithered on her belly
through wet and slick or
dry and rocky tubes
out into crystal caverns
she saw dimly in the beam
of her solitary flashlight —

her dread at getting lost there
in her solitary sojourn —
then how she emerged
wet and dirty —
covered in glitter —
to a sun-filled afternoon.

You fell into a sinkhole once
on this mountain,
when you were a little girl.
You slid down the slope,
lay stunned at the bottom,
breath knocked out of you.
It took hard scrabbling
with sore scraped hands
to crawl your way out.

Piano Music

When your mother plays the piano,
it is like a conversation in a restaurant
where the waiter has forgotten you,
but you do not notice.
An hour passes, and then another.
Your mother's fingers sweep across the keys.
You find that you are no longer hungry.

Fake Flowers I

One year
your mother got tired
of planting her garden.

She bought
a dozen red silk roses
a dozen yellow silk tulips
and a dozen blue iris.
She planted them
along her front walk
alternating colors
with some silk ferns
to fill in between.

You didn't see them yourself,
but every time you went to town
you heard about them.
By the time you went to see her
it was autumn
and she'd pulled them all up.

Two Rivers

You walk up the trail that leads
to your mother's house, the one
high above on this mountainside.

You walk steadily now you've learned
the careful step of age and the popping
in the knees. You see your mother's hands

on her own knees complaining of the cold.
You take the bridge over those two rivers,
winter's not the time to ford them

and they will be there whether you
wade through them or watch them
from above. You loop back around

to where they've come together and made
one placid body flowing, smooth as glass.
You know your mother will be home.

Rock face

On this mountain there is a granite cliff
that stretches for hundreds of yards
along the path that goes around and up
towards your mother's house.

The path goes along the bottom
then winds around along the top
of this solid rock face,

from below it is a fortress.
You can't imagine that it could ever fall
although rocks sometimes crumble —
you find them along
the path in front of you or see them
rolled further down the slope below.

From the top of the cliff,
all you can see is space
falling away.

Light everywhere evenly at once

Your mother looks at the light
dawning through the trees.
She sits at her kitchen table,
sips coffee black no sugar —
the light is everywhere
evenly at once present
in all the places dim.

Your mother thinks about you
down on the back side
of the mountain
still in its shadow.

She wonders if you have
risen in the dark,
if you sip your coffee
milk no sugar
on a hard chair
at your kitchen table
lit by lamps.

Night

Here on this mountain the sounds are strange —
the snuffling rustling of small creatures
in the leaves, the call of owls first here
then far away, flying a wide range,
the crunches of something bigger,
the rattle of the garbage cans.

These nights you wonder
how your mother fares.
Is she still putting sugar water
out for hummingbirds?
Is she still in the habit
of feeding bears?

Panes

When your mother was your age
she lived alone, like you do.
She walked everywhere
and never drove,
you don't know where she went.

For you, always interruptions—
a crossword clue
you can't figure,
the cat at the door,
the radio alarm,
a mockingbird or blue jay
raucous in the yard.

At your age, you never walk.
Your body is antique glass
melting down to the bottom.

Stairs daunt you,
but you take them
four times daily.

Your mother owns the mountaintop,
never has to worry about her view.
In your yard the bushes have all grown tall
your view is narrower each summer.

In your house it's the same—
trails are starting to form,
the open spaces filling up.

Stones

She wanted to know   she asked
not long before she died   you answered
fingers over your mouth   your voice
muffled

Forgiveness is a slow slow turn
of many rocks or the same one rolled
again and again   a painstaking look
at the veins of quartz
a test of surface with tongue
see what shines   the dirt and bits
of leaves brought in   the tang of
swallowed grit   between the teeth
the crunch   brittle in the ears

It takes a lot of wary cleaning
the watchful piling up of many stones
to understand all of what you forgive
and whom

Alice Teeter is a Lecturer in Poetry at Emory University in Atlanta, Georgia. She studied poetry at Eckerd College with Peter Meinke and her chapbook *20 CLASS A* was published in 1975 by Morningstar Media. Her collection of poems String Theory won the Georgia Poetry Society's 2008 Charles B. Dickson Chapbook Contest. Her poetry collection *When It Happens To You . . .* was published in 2009 by Star Cloud Press, and Elephant Girls was published in 2015 by Aldrich.

Teeter is a member of Alternate ROOTS, a service organization for artists at the intersection of arts and activism in the Southeast; a member of the Artist Conference Network, a national coaching community for people doing creative work; and a member of the Atlanta Women's Poetry Collective. She performs regularly with the Imprah!vables, a local theatrical improv troupe and co-leads, with Lesly Fredman, Improvoetry workshops that combine poetry writing and theatrical improv.

www.ingramcontent.com/pod-product-compliance
Lightning Source LLC
LaVergne TN
LVHW041519070426
835507LV00012B/1691